The Walled Wife

The Walled WIFE

poems

NICELLE DAVIS

 RED HEN PRESS | PASADENA, CA

Book layout by Hannah Nelson & Latina Vidolova

Library of Congress Cataloging-in-Publication Data

Names: Davis, Nicelle (Nicelle Christine), 1979– author.
Title: The walled wife / Nicelle Davis.
Description: First edition. | Pasadena, CA : Red Hen Press, [2016]
Identifiers: LCCN 2015046625 | ISBN 9781597097253 (softcover)
Subjects: | BISAC: POETRY / American / General.
Classification: LCC PS3604.A97268 A6 2016 | DDC 811/.6—dc23
LC record available at http://lccn.loc.gov/2015046625

The National Endowment for the Arts, the Los Angeles County Arts Commission, the
Pasadena Arts & Culture Commission and the City of Pasadena Cultural Affairs Division,
the Los Angeles Department of Cultural Affairs, the Dwight Stuart Youth Fund, Sony
Pictures Entertainment, and the Ahmanson Foundation partially support Red Hen Press.

First Edition
Published by Red Hen Press
www.redhen.org

Acknowledgments

Grateful acknowledgment is made to the editors of the publications in which these poems first appeared, some in earlier forms: *A cappella Zoo*: "First Night In the Wall" and "The Second Night Continues"; *Bayou Magazine*: "Respond Only with Parenthetical Exceptions," "The Wife Advises Rada the Builder: We Are Desperate for Answers"; *Gargoyle*: "Foot Note 2," "Foot Note 3," and "Foot Note 5"; *Manor House Quarterly*: "As a Story Goes: Structurally," "The First Hour Of Being Buried Alive In the Walls Of A Half-Built Cathedral," "Theorem 51: The Diagonals of a Rectangle are Equal," and "Third Hour of Being Buried Alive, The Wife Thinks of Her Last Day in Church: Or Sharp Edges Hidden In A Seamstress Dress"; *The Santa Fe Lit Review*: "She Tells You."

This book is dedicated to my cellmate Kate Gale.

Special thanks to Adam Smith, whose countless hours of editorial advice helped form the architecture of this collection.

Contents

WALL 1 : CASE STUDIES

WALL 4 : MARGINALIA

THE WALLED WIFE

The Teller, The Listener, The Tale:
An Introduction to *The Walled Wife*

We are shaped by story. Narratives tell us who we are, where we came from, what we believe, who we can become. They tell us what is worth fighting and dying for. They tell us who to revere and who to revile. They tell us how to be good, describe the consequence of evil, play out for us through plot the domino effect of one decision upon another. They often seem simpler than they are, though the best stories unfold for us the complexities of our human condition, the waywardness of our desires, the grace we are capable of, and yet fall short of over and over. If we're lucky, they offer us a possible path to redemption.

That's a lot of power.

And so it's no surprise that writers are drawn back and back to the stories around us. On the one hand, because of their foundational world-making work, we cling to stories for their continuity, for the ways that they remind us of the givens of our cultures and societies. On the other hand, because our possibilities are always changing, in different times, places, and stages of cultural evolution, we revisit the narratives that construct our worldviews, hold them up to a contemporary light to see what endures, and what needs revision. A possible mission for the writer, should she choose to accept it, is to refract inherited narratives, to shift the lenses and make us see them anew.

This is exactly what Nicelle Davis does in the poems that comprise *The Walled Wife*.

"The Ballad of the Walled-Up Wife," is a poem/song/narrative that has survived across several centuries and cultures in Eastern Europe. According to Alan Dundes, who compiled an anthology of critical scholarship on this ballad, it is one of the most prevalent and most studied ballads in that part of the world (*The Walled-Up Wife*, vii-viii). Though there is a diversity of plot and circumstance, the basic movement of the tale remains constant, and contains the depressingly familiar tropes of many narratives related to women— love, betrayal, sacrifice, motherhood, surrender, and death.

The version of the ballad with which this collection concerns itself goes like this: it's believed that a woman must be buried within the walls of edifices in order for the buildings to stand. The master builder, Rada, is building a citadel, Skadar, and asks the three kings to send one of their wives— he wants a powerful woman—to make the citadel strong. The three kings make a secret pact that whichever wife brings lunch the next day will be the sacrifice. Two of the brothers renege on the promise, and tell their wives. Thus, the youngest wife is tricked into being immured. She begs to have a window left that she could suckle her infant son. And she does, until she dies.

In the poems of *The Walled Wife*, Davis introduces this ancient folksong to our contemporary narrative landscape. The poems serve as a primary text, a retelling of the story in verse, much like the tradition of the ballad itself. There is a satisfaction—primal and powerful—in the masterful and dramatic revelation of action in these poems, as well as in the wonderfully wrought characters Davis is able to construct in her poems. Consider this excerpt from "In Some Versions, the Husband Sends a Bird to Save His Wife," in which the reader both sees the action, the impending consequence, and the king's emotional condition as he, too, watches the story unfurl:

> "He watches, perched in a tree, undignified as a god's eye;
> desperation makes birds of even kings. He watches her
> come—with every step, he sees Yahweh killing his queen.
>
> . . .
>
> He chokes back his tongue, trying to form a response—
> the bird in his mouth writhes . . ."

The poems' fluid perspective, which gives depth to all of the players within the narrative, defies a single narrating voice, a move that both deepens the tale, and simultaneously reconstructs it. First and foremost, we experience the consciousness of the Wife, and it is her voice, her needs, hungers, etc. that the poems concern themselves with, locating this collection of poems firmly within a feminist tradition of removing women's voices from the sidelines. The wife is not merely the subject of the ballad, nor is she the aesthetic object she's constructed to be in the story; instead, she is a subjective perspective from which the narrative emerges, and thus, she is given the power of voice and visibility not present in the original ballad.

A great example lies in the final stanza of the original ballad, the first few lines of which read thus:

> "The slender bride was then immured
> Her cradled son was brought to her,

And he did nurse a week of days,
After a week her voice was gone . . .”

Compare the excerpt above to the last lines of Davis' "The First Hour Of Being Buried Alive in the Walls Of A Half-Built Cathedral":

"I feel

        my voice,

    a stone,

        I threw long ago, but windows
continue crashing

as an indefinable

        light, exits from me."

From the objective storyteller of the first version, we are offered only plot—action that moves the story along; however, by inhabiting the perspective of the wife, Davis is able to also explore/explode the action. The move to inhabit the wife's perspective not only intensifies the action, but gives her the power to name her experience. This is not a reclamation of agency within the story—the plot doesn't change—but a refraction of power within the world of the text, which then shifts how the text is/can be received.

Also present in the multiple perspectives is the persona of the authorial/narrating voice. There is an "I" here telling the story, and that, too, is treated as a dimension of the text that must be made visible. Moreover, it is clear throughout the poems that this speaker is not simply interested in narrative unfolding, but in removing the layer of "observer" altogether, and acknowledging the fact that to speak the story is to have another kind of power. This is perhaps clearest in the poem "This Part Doesn't Actually Happen In *the Ballad of the Walled-up Wife*, but I punish the queens anyway," where in a moment of radical transparency, the narrative voice of the poems' speaker surges through, letting the readers know that she is not detached, but on the contrary, both present and invested in the story she is recounting. Moreover, she both points out and wields this speaking power, and aligns it with the character of the wife, thereby showing and redressing a moral/ethical deficiency within the story.

This radical transparency also allows us to see the speaking voice as imperfect. Sometimes this is humorous, as in the poem "On the Third Day, I Lose the Case Study." However, more powerfully, this is demonstrated in the first person lyric poems that are interspersed with the wife's narrative throughout the collection. These poems work to reveal the teller as vulnerable, intensely human, flawed—a being far from the more common omniscient and infallible authorial voice of folklore. Moreover, this move highlights the very reason we turn to story—to make meaning of our own lives. The narrative voice confesses in "My Little Box Head Responds/Objects to Found Poetry and the Rewriting of *The Ballad of the Walled-up Wife*" "I thought I would dig her up but/I only uncovered my desire to be brought down, to be bound." And later, in another section of the same poem, she writes, "The wife became my architecture for search," brilliantly demonstrating the cyclical truth inherent in narrative—stories arise from a need that only stories can satisfy.

Because it not only takes the text of the ballad, but also critical responses to the text as its axis, Davis' collection also expands the function of her poems to secondary as well as primary text. By grounding every poem with a contextual epigraph from the critical realm—in almost every case, Alan Dundes' book, *The Walled-up Wife: A Casebook*—there is a meta-commentary at work here, reminding us that this text is also aware of itself as text and as such, should not be merely absorbed, but critiqued, examined, and interpreted.

"Interviewing Two Girls Age 10 and 8 About Being Buried Alive" shows that this awareness is not only present, but essential, and poignantly models how this critical questioning might occur:

> **"Would you let someone bury you alive for love?**
> 8: Hmmmm . . . no no
> 10: No
>
> **The mom interrupts the interview:**
>
> That's creepy, but if I think about it,
> I guess I'm already buried alive; but only by him; It could only be for him."

This critical poetics furthers the implicit claim of the collection: the teller of story is not a neutral space to inhabit in the transaction of meaning, and neither is the position of audience/listener/

receiver. This approach shows how we might all critically engage in the mythologies that surround us, and moreover, how ideas values and beliefs hidden in story might slip into the fabric of our worldview unnoticed and unchallenged if we don't interrogate them, hold them up to a critical light.

The poems in this collection also take on language itself. Like the walls of the building that trap the body, voice and life of the wife, language itself has often bricked up, muffled and obscured women's voices. And so, on the most fundamental level, the poems challenge structure, taking on this reclamation of voice in their very construction. The poems concern themselves with gaps and space on the page, making visible both absence (of agency? of voice? of value?) and silence in their use of white space. However, the use of space also opens the poems, provides room within the narrative for reflection, and carves a place for the reader to dwell within the linguistic structure of the poem—to become the wife, and not just the words that bury her.

Visually, the poems are often dynamic: they stream, slither, and fracture—now as orderly as a row of trees, now as chaotic as leaves in the wind. This mobility, this refusal of fixity, destabilizes our expectation of well-behaved verse, and in this disruption, creates fissures through which other meanings and experiences can enter the narrative. In addition, the array of form and textual tools— from footnotes, italics, and play with font and margin, to concrete poetry, interviews, and prose poems—not only keeps readers agile and engaged, but also mirrors the central tensions of voice and embodiment in the poems.

While the myth of "the Walled-up Wife" is ancient, the true myth here is that we've not heard this story before, or that it's not a story that resonates in the present cultural landscape as much as it did in Eastern Europe centuries ago. Buried in the ballad is a host of issues that continue to plague women in the contemporary world: the woman's body as sacrifice; the woman's body as tender or currency; the woman's body as disposable; the woman's body as property; the woman's body as aesthetic object; the woman's body unsafe in the world she must inhabit, and in the hands of the people she loves.

In the baldest terms, the ballad is about a woman's murder hidden under the guise of duty and sacrifice; the resolution/redemption occurs as the wife, surrendering to her fate, selflessly mothers her son with the last her body has to give:

> "After a week, her voice was gone,
> But for her child there still was milk:
> She nursed him for a year of days!"

And indeed, there is a reward for this sacrifice:

> "As it was then, so it is now,
> Today, as then, the milk does flow,
> It works great wonders and great cures,
> For every woman with no milk."

However, the structure and content of Davis' poems offers a potent challenge to this maternal, martyrly conclusion, and the subtexts of the narrative itself (see above).

The project of retelling itself is critiqued in "My Little Box Head Responds/Objects to Found Poetry and the rewriting of 'The Ballad of the Walled-up Wife,'" with the question, *Your point is?* To answer, I posit that in unearthing "this fucked-up story," Davis' poems remind us that narratives, like the individuals and cultures that produce them, are imperfect structures. However, through her intelligent and effective use of craft and voice, and the heartbreaking vulnerability with which she engages the perspectives within and without the story, Davis avoids simple replication; she does not "rebuild a corrupt structure." Rather, she exhibits the powerful and expansive possibilities of narrative. This collection makes space (in the narrative, and thus in the reader, and thus in the culture) for so much—for remorse from the builder, for sorrow from the husband, but mostly for this sacrificed woman to be angry, to feel betrayed, to be avenged, to tend to her inner life in the hours of her death, to speak her truth, and insist on her humanity. These poems allow the wife to mourn her stolen life, and as we mourn with her, they enrich our possibilities for empowerment and empathy in the narratives of our lives.

—Lauren K. Alleyne

Wall 1

Case Studies:

Pick the book up next to you; see how it assimilates with the lost text—one plot bleeds into the next—effortlessly. Find yourself in a mirror; analogize your selves—seep into the next—

As a Story Goes: Structurally

Although the practice of offering a human sacrifice on laying the foundations of a building was intended
originally as a propitiation of the spirits of the earth, who were thought of as being disturbed, later on it
sometimes passed into another conception, that the spirit of the victim would be a ghostly guardian of the
building being erected.

—Paul G. Brewster, "The Foundations Sacrifice Motif," *The Walled-Up Wife: A Casebook*

Story begins with
eldest, middle, youngest.
Kings—
magic by division
of threes.

emp / ti / ness—
worth / less / ness—

rooms must be
filled with

sac / ri / fice—

One merged to
a king will
do,

the *vila*[1]
calls: *bury
her and at once
the church will rise.*

As the Story Continues, Red Stains in White Linens

In a variant from Trebizond the master mason hears a voice asking him: "What will you give me to keep the wall from falling again?" He answers: "Mother and daughter I can have no longer, but wife I can and perhaps I shall find a better one."

—Mircea Eliade, "Master Manole and the Monastery of Arges," *The Walled-Up Wife: A Casebook*

The three agree not to tell—let the first arriving wife
be buried. The eldest king warns his wife, *don't come—
the construction site—will kill you,* says the middle king.

The youngest king confesses nothing. Married to fate—
he prays to god and lays down with their baby between
them; a wall of new flesh bars his hands from touching

his wife. Full moon, the world shines as a blue-tinted
day. He can't sleep. Come morning, the youngest wife
goes to her sisters, who tell her they are sick with a pain

that cannot heal. They ask, *bring the men their meals.* Theirs
plus hers—three times a regular load, she objects: *But I
must² bathe my infant son, must wash his fine white clothes, must*

The queens reply: *My dear young sister, go at once, / And
bring the men their daily meal. / For we will wash your son's
white clothes, / And bathe with care your infant son.*

In Some Versions, the Husband Sends a Bird to Save His Wife

Her love and devotion cannot be contained; they exceed all measure, outdo even the forces of the Divine and the Supernatural. And once more the irony is superb, for her extraordinary power for love and faith-fulness is at once the greatest force within the poem, and the cause of the hero and heroine's downfall.

—Sharon King, "Beyond the Pale," *The Walled-Up Wife: A Casebook*

He watches, perched in a tree, undignified as god's eye;
desperation makes birds of even kings. He watches her
come—with every step, he sees Yahweh killing his queen.

With betrayal, he returns to the old magi. His tongue trans-
forms to a robin. He flies to her—red breast heaving—
Don't go. Don't go. Don't. The color to please rises in her as

flesh presses. Onward. He begs, this time to the river. But
she risks drowning believing effort will make him love her
more. The river overflows—she swells against going under.

Again. He asks for winds to beat on her from all directions.
But she pushes through to the construction site. On arrival,
she calls out, *Love?* Repeats *love*, when he doesn't answer.

He chokes back his tongue, trying to form a response—
the bird in his mouth writhes. *Have faith,* he tells her. *But
it is difficult,* she cries. He assures her, *it wouldn't be faith*[3]

if it were easy.

23

We Say, We See, Holes in the Chapel's Construction: The Youngest Wife Helps Her Husband Bury Her Alive

"... the wall presses me too hard and crushes my weeping breast and breaks my child and my life is failing."

—"Master Manole and the Monastery of Arges," *The Walled-Up Wife: A Casebook*

Go after the glint, your   fingers' motion like wings   after wedding bands,

reflecting sunlight,   casting stars   against a darkness

in half-built rooms. *Go down,* repeats. The building   crew watches, holding

their hammers like stillborns to their chests. It matters little what I say. *No,* is

what our son said   as I left   to bring you lentils.

Tastes like you, you'd say. Our son   and   you nestled upon   your   own breast

of me. Lowering myself   between   wall frames—masons pour mortar. *Stand*

still, you say.   *Won't be long,* I told   our son with-

out looking back.   *Look at me,*   I say—before you knock me dim—I hear our

son crying,   but it's your face   I see   weeping over   the red bricks[4] that stack

against me.

THE LITTLEST WIFE WAKES HALF-BURIED IN THE CHAPEL'S WALLS

The woman stands for the food carrier: she brings victuals and suckles her baby therefore sustains and grows life. She prepares the food and feeds on her own substance—milk: eventually she will become the complete food of the work initiated by the male brotherhood, when she is swallowed by the wall.

—Serban Anghelescu, "The Wall and the Water," *The Walled-Up Wife: A Casebook*

Birds   below me.   Not

birds.   Eyes.[5]   I realize.

I am crying into another

man.   *Please*. A window.

For my son. A   door. To

feed from. My breast. An

opening.

Rada the Builder

The master proclaims the possibility of movement, of multiplicity and progress. He contests the existence of the limit and of the center because of a dominant anxiety—exhaustion—ruling him. Unlike all the other masons, the master, who "excels masons young and old / His heart like ice cold," is defined from the very beginning by an inherent oxymoron, one consubstantial with his personality, by virtue of opposites (mobile/immobile, warm/cold) coinciding. Warm like blood, milk, and tears; cold like stone.

—Serban Anghelescu, "The Wall and the Water," *The Walled-Up Wife: A Casebook*

She asks for a door.[6]

I give that.

She asks for a window.

I give that too.

But no more. Enough—
enough.

Any more and
the church
will fall.

The First Hour of Being Buried Alive in the Walls of a Half-Built Cathedral

Since death and events surrounding it are considered dangerous, it follows that those who directly deal with death both court danger and are dangerous. And, accompanying this dangerous status of women is power.

—Ruth Mandel, "Sacrifice at the Bridge of Arta," *The Walled-Up Wife: A Casebook*

A sky
       is eaten by clouds.

A ceiling
       drops as shattered glass.

A tree
       shakes from standing for flocks of feet.

A wall
       is screaming as birds will yell—

A unified
       cry before migration.

       What was said—black bird to brown bird? What was it I saw?
A dirt path—

       curious objects? Finches copulating while
a cat

       swallows them. Fists for bodies,
they never

stop beating upon each
other—rhythms

implying melody—pounding to open
themselves

like doors. Finality.
I feel
my voice,
a stone,

I threw long ago, but windows
continue crashing

as an indefinable[7]
light, exits from me.

Blood Price: Hot in the Hole, the Wife Is Given Water

A violent death, a sacrifice, begets creativity.

—Ruth Mandel, "Sacrifice at the Bridge of Arta," *The Walled-Up Wife: A Casebook*

The house built of me

from crushed fox bones

wants to bite your cock

like a bird's neck, flesh

tresses snapped in two,

but I refuse to be teeth.

You hand me a cup of

water through the little

door at my nipple line.

Drink, you say. I drink.

I drink 'til drunk.[8]

FLESH PRICE

The fidelity of a people to one or another mythical scenario, to one or another exemplary image, tells us far
more about its deeper soul than many of its historical accomplishments.

—Mircea Eliade, "Master Manole and the Monastery of Arges," *The Walled-Up Wife: A Casebook*

A girl brings my son to suckle
at the small door in the wall. Promise

agitates him. He bites my tits until I'm bleeding—
chokes on the salt of me—cries from anger instead

of sorrow. I fade further into the bones of me. Like water
into ground. A nursemaid takes him. I'm nearly all absorbed.

A girl is crying a name I once dressed in, but
her voice is a river—all movement. She is not

a shore I know
how to cling to.[9]

Dripping with Liquid Flesh: Parts of an Egg

But the idea of a Center through which the axis mundi passes and which, in consequence, makes communication between Sky and Earth possible is also found at a still earlier stage of culture.

—Mircea Eliade, "Master Manole and the Monastery of Arges," *The Walled-Up Wife: A Casebook*

Shell: There is no daughter; the girl is the wife.

This is to say:
there is no escape; there is only permitting
the younger-self back in.

Albumin: Open yourself like an egg—let flight fall
from your fingers.

Say the word
yolk and hear how it sounds like yoke—

Yolk: This girl believes in you—who will believe in her?[10]

The Earliest Recorded Version of "The Walled-Up Wife"

Dundes said he sometimes finds it hard to account for the enduring popularity of "The Walled-Up Wife"
since it is such a sad song.

—Gretchen Kell, University of California, Berkeley News Release, 1997

Kavadzic: sends it

      Grimm: it is

            Goethe: it shouldn't be

Kavadzic: save it

      Grimm: is it

            Goethe: shouldn't be it

Kavadzic: but we are it

      Grimm: and shouldn't be

            Goethe: the barbarity of it

      Grimm: must know it to kill it

            Goethe: say it and it is, no matter how much
you kill it.

Kavadzic: does it matter what it is
does it
so long as there is song
to combat the implications
of all this impending stillness[11]

Notes from Page 36

The Supporting Evidence

The rebuilding of Jericho:
    foundations drown a first-born with
    the weight of gates upon a youngest

For the Hampi Wall:
    she is pregnant; the two are alive in one,
    when earth folds over the screaming gaps

Hooghly Bridge 1872:
    on record, fear a form of belief—
    an arch demands a layer of skulls

A few examples of:
    slave girls in a hole—slave girls as hole
    first pole of home chimes the bones

Also:
    child in this and that castle because
    mothers sell "it" for the purpose

Testimony
    skeletons in the walls—a world within the cell. This
    is why we still count our offspring by their heads.[12]

On the Third Day, I Lose the Case Study

Damn it, where is that book about the book?[13]

{ Wall 2

Foot Notes:

If You are the Wife in the Wall, You are More so the Builder Immuring Her.
Postulate: The *You* and *I* are now understood to be interchangeable.

Footnote #1 (vila):

A Calling: for sacrifice

A *port*—an ending.

Or is it?
The *people* call:
            for beyond.

Now with definition, *vila*:
a haven—
with a defined end—
yet implications of beyond.

            a [live]
As she is buried [alive] structure is born.
            a [   ] live

Footnote #2 (must):

This Part Doesn't Actually Happen *in the* "Ballad of the Walled-Up Wife," but I punish the queens anyway

The littlest sister leaves; her baby cries. Eventually, the sisters swaddle him to near collapse. He can barely breathe, much less bawl himself to sleep. By the time his mother is buried alive—his clothes are soaked in excrement—his skin covered in a rash. His wraps come off as bloody skin. Washing the boy, eldest sister will lose control of her senses—the scent of oranges making her vomit. Empty self. Dressing the child, middle sister will begin to stutter. Their heads split open when in light.

These women *must*

know life   through

objects—   only seeing

children   if children

are holding   gold & silver.

Children say,   *I have brought*

you the moon   *—the sun.*

Now sleep,   *Mommy, sleep.*

Day and night   *will go on with*   *out you. You are not*

to blame

for rotations.

I wonder, if not the sisters, who is to blame?

Footnote #3 (faith):

Interviewing Two Girls, Ages 10 and 8, About Being Buried Alive

Do you believe in love?
> 10: Yes.
> 8: Yes.

Why?
> 10: Because it's evident. Everyone loves each other. I can see it.

How do you see it—what is your evidence?
> 8: Because . . . hmm . . . hmm . . . more people come into the world.
> 10: If no one loved each other, there wouldn't be babies, and without babies
> there would be no evolution—
> > but, eh, I don't want to say the word for how
> > babies are made.

That word you won't say, does it mean the same thing as love?
> 10: Yes.
> 8: I don't know what you're talking about.

Why is evolution important?
> 10: Evolution's not really important; what is important is learning. With thinking, we
> won't spend our lives saying, *god made the world*. You can't just follow what your
> parents say; they may have gone on the wrong websites. Or even worse, parents may
> have gotten their evidence from their parents, who didn't have all the info. The future
> will know more than any of us.
> 8: I agree, because if all of us were just saying god stuff, we wouldn't be focusing on
> what we need to. Praying is like talking to no one. Meditation just makes you feel
> relaxed, but if you pray for an A on a math test, the next day you might get an F
> and feel bad. Praying makes people feel bad.

Would you let someone bury you alive for love?
> 8: Hmmm . . . no no.
> 10: No.

The mom interrupts the interview:

That's creepy, but if I think about it,

I guess I'm already buried alive; but only by him. It could only be for him.

What does your mom mean by that?

10: She loves her husband so much she would let him bury her in books.

8: Yes, I think he would bury her in little bits of bookshelves.

If you had to be buried alive, what would you be buried in?

8: Maybe Legos, maybe. Maybe, I would let love bury me in Legos.

10: (loudly) I want to live; what is the point of being alive if you are just going to die.

You know we are all going to die? Right?

The mom interrupts:

Dinner is ready. Do you want greens?

FOOTNOTE #4 (BRICKS):

Theorem 51:   The Diagonals   of a Rectangle   Are Equal

Euclid, meaning *Good Glory, Good* from the root *gothaz* meaning *belonging together*, and *Glory* approximating an expression of brightness   (to clarify, *brightness*, as in not the light of a candle, but its shine),   fathers geometry in 300 BC.   Axiom: a needed assumption—a truth taken for granted, to serve as starting point for deduction, for inferring other (theory dependent) truths. A brick, diagonals of a rectangle congruent, will stack to make a structurally sound building. Bodies mimicking the whole structure. The blueprint of faith implemented in stories.

FOOTNOTE #5 (EYES):

The eye shape is as we imagine. A section inside
that comes out. Then circles, perfect to whatever
degree you are able. Highlight the suggestions of
a window in a wall providing light. Lashes of a
female. At the bottom, make a shelf of flesh be-
fore shading the lower wings. Realism requires:
Reference. Patience. Time. Life drawing demands
a building of dark and light: depths of shadows.

There is
something in   the shape
of   the
eye   that
suggests . . .   that is,
the shading   of an eye
might   *(my only remaining prayer:*   suggest . . .
dare   I
suggest . . .   *let there be*   there is
something   *something)*   in the eye
that   says
we   are
designed   to
not   just
look,   but see
each   other?
There is
something—

(please, something)

FOOTNOTE #6 (DOOR):

Make the shape
of empty, a vaginal
room. Put her in it;
let   it   consume
her—this effigy of
our   first   felt
rejection, the womb
who no longer wants
us. Turn her body
into a door—let us
enter and exit at will.

Footnote #7 (indefinable):

I.

I compare variations of a song sung across the globe. Lyrics go: a wife is buried so a structure can rise—it implies a room is worth more than a woman and as a place she approximates value. I look at my small home and think how few enter. I sing the "Ballad of the Walled-Up Wife" for days without sleeping; the rhythm bruises my lamps. In a shade, I watch an egg burst into a million fanged stars; spiderlings secrete silver and fall. Their footed arms fingering me, I rethink home as a world of infinite entrances.

II.

Studying the architecture of Kinbaku knots, I attempt to bind flesh into the shape of a bird—alternatives for flight—bound suspension. Singing allows my voice to walk through walls, so again I sing. Again wonder, how much of my life will be lived as an albatross? It's impossible to move with these dark wings gyrating; I come undone to look at stars who will never touch me with the weight of house spiders. The sky lowers itself in unbounded layers; I am no place—nothing.

III.

Let's give the wife a name, let's say it's Cassandra. Sound of loose change: shake it. *Ca-ca-ca* it goes; *ca-ca-ca* I go. Like crows. On days I feel wings in my purse—a sexual im-im-pulsiveness—I keep to books: read prophecies no one will believe. Close covers and flip for faces—foresight coming down in staccatos. Dropping change I count yes, count denial. Admit: untouchable—I live solely for the chance to be held by what hates me. Hysteric. The little girl inside me is crying. She holds a knife. I could cut her neck by thinking it, but it's hard to think with her howling. She holds the knife against me. *Ca-ca-ca* she crows. *Ca-ca-ca* the knife goes. Red pennies fall from heaven. Look, to the ground—there is the story of how we fail each other.

Footnote #8 (drunk):

Once the Wife and Girl Become One, a Language (Unlike Words)
    Appears upon the Wall, as seen in

Vuk Karadzic: Footnote #8: An Incomplete Rendering:
( ) Indicates Slight Alterations

People say liquid oozes from	(her)	wall—
	(she)	the hole
through which the	son	nursed.

Women—mix this chalk with water. Drink it.
Women   who   cannot   nurse.
Women who cannot bear the pain of fullness.

(a row of women licking stone—bringing onto
themselves a standing strength—taste of
birthed desire—into selves
a prayer to be enough—
knowing prayer is
not enough.)

Footnote #9 (cling to):

In me is a little girl I've locked away.
When she tries to escape I slap her
face until palms bleed, that is to say
I sing myself to sleep when her tears
surface on our face. When we face
each other I tell her to shut the fuck
up before they find us—they who
will do more than hurt her—they
who will break her entirely of song.
When we sing, we sing to be birds
to fly beyond hands and unto eye
shot—those bullets that burst hearts
into origin rhythms. There is
freedom in being seen without
hands breaking wings. She believes
in everyone—will hand wings over
to any palm to prove we are better
than bleeding. I believe in her, only.
Only her I keep from going blood
dry—safe in other—she's in place.
In me is a little girl I've locked away.

Domestication: A Recipe

The experimenter attempts to handle her while offering food.
Noted: a preference for other
foxes, or humans. After a fox reaches sexual maturity there
is an overall tameness score.
Among test factors: approachability, bite, touch. By way
of ensuring genetic obedience,
foxes are not subjected to any training and permitted
only brief contact with people.
These behavioral changes come with physical
alterations: red coats fade to
grey. Behavior by controlled breeding:
see the bitch wag her tail?
You want more reason for burning
a vixen? The tame bred
also lose their musky smell.

FOOTNOTE #11 (STILLNESS):

Circles: This is not retelling—

this is the daughter I'll never have.

A halfway point,

a reference for regret.

Inside / Outside

interchangeable. Admit—

I—is created from what will never be.

Footnote #12 (heads):

Double Identity: If You are Interchangeable with I, We Can Become No-thing: Notes from Frank Close's *Nothing*

Was there below?

> Aristotelian logic: nature abhors a vacuum. This was regarded as self-evident; nonetheless it was dead wrong (9).

Was there above?

> Robert Hooke: makes vacuum pumps. He proves the disappearance of air by suffocating birds (17).

What stirred? Where?

> Pascal noted: air is the cause of all the phenomena philosophers attribute to an "imaginary cause" (21).

Stirring:

> Marginalia: *it was wrong—suffocating birds—imagining causes.*

FOOTNOTE #13 (BOOK):

Bloody-egg, a bird is calling you, hear it sing:

> These stories will destroy us—why do you let them
> make a house of us? We are lock. We are key. Turn
> the knob that belongs to no door. Come in. In here
>
> is other—you turned to I, I turned to you. There are
> worlds within worlds. The story written on our faces
> will save us, but you must turn towards the forth wall—
>
> let the audience becomes yoke, the stage shell, be-
> hind you the wings are resting on a foundation of
> bones. Excavate to find escape. You are always wel-
>
> come inside me.

girl

Inside:

How does a bird fly without sky?

Respond Only with Parenthetical Exceptions

(This is you: the hole   in a hole   holding. Remember
how your son shot like a bullet—   life tearing your
perineum to get out—   of wall   —of womb. You were
instructed to wait,   so you waited.   You waited.   You.
Waited for the doctor, who stitched your crotch while telling the
other—*I added extra butterflies—you'll*
thank me for the tightness.)

(This is nothing in comparison to your sisters:

with self-defense instructor as sexual predator,

bruises rearticulated with knives,

seventeen stabs—the third strike fatal,

a mouth swollen closed,

eyes blued shut.

Nothing in comparison to the whole.)

(Remember
your son's lasting image of you
is *waiting.*)

There Are More Exceptions: She Tells You

For my thirteenth birthday, I bought a lock
to keep my father out.

My Little Box Head Responds / Objects to Found Poetry and the Rewriting of "The Ballad of the Walled-Up Wife"

I. Stop being so fucking clever poet: *here, the blueprint:*

What I found in "The Wife" is this: I thought I would dig her up, but
I only uncovered my desire to be brought down, to be bound.

      II. A Friend Criticizes: *I've listened to you go on about this for hours.*

      Enough. Don't you think this is out of time—we are past this?
      You only love patriarchy because it's familiar; why retell this
      fucked-up story? Why rebuild a corrupt structure? *Your point is?*

III. What I Can't Explicitly Say in *Italics: I seldom feel human.*

I can't distinguish love from a desire to be named. Confession:
*I feel less like a grave when a he says my name. As death approaches, I fuck
like a shovel, as though this were my way out of the grave.* I watch his eyes
to see if anyone's capable of loving *not just any grave, but this name.*
I don't want to be saved. *I want to feel like my little life is worthy of
this question*—I watch his eyes to see if he will, *ask for my name.*

      IV. The point

      The wife became my architecture for search. This is not
      the same as being saved. This is not the same as being re-
      named or claimed. What I need to find is beyond walls,
      past definition. Call it something—something indefinable as . . .

V.　…*Love*

　　　anymore
　　　only trans-
　　　lates to shame.

I have a name; I am / am not ashamed of it.

EXPERIMENTS IN BEING BURIED

I. Alive in Naked Earth

Holding shovel is a boy—not boy so much as a body growing.
How his skin—patch of ground—is like a bed. What can't be
sown in youth? Clean well mouth—spring of throat. New. My

skin's a stained sheet tied to a dry-line. I've asked him, to *fold &*
bury me? He'll do as instructed. Spade corner to garden corner.
Hands of earth against my mouth—there was a time I believed

in the all-consuming. I want to believe again. Holding a shovel,
is a boy. Buried alive, I reclaim something:

> *remember when love smelled like rain?*

II. Buried Alive in Cinder Block

My students build me into
tower. Standing for three
hours, reading old texts aloud,
I have no idea what they are
doing on the other side of me.
Eventually they pull back the
bricks to reveal graffiti. A girl
who cannot hear, has drawn a
sun in sunglasses. The man in
charge of safety admits: *I*
enjoyed that: I really did. Truth
told, so do I. Isn't this the
story we've longed for?
Babel—that universal reach

towards something larger
than self. I ask what's
remembered; and no one
knows *what* to say. Or is it

     how to say . . .

III. Masturbating in Someone Else's Bed

I'm not home when he begins to ignore me; I hold my breath until blinded
by asphyxiation. I'm again void. Again, invisible. Light. It's all heat now. I
turn towards myself; she has our face in our hands. She's pounding it into
the ground. As sky snatches ocean, held high, she drops me. A skyline fall.
Covered in blood, I come—sobbing with the automatic song of pleasure—my
fingers red stains—robins fluttering over broken eggs—their wings sound
    the question, *Why? Why? Why?*

TURNFALKEN AND RAVENS

I pay too much to ride the *Express* for a one-night stand with London.
From 10 p.m. to 5 a.m. I walk church to church. The straps of my
carry-on cutting into my shoulders, by morning I'm bleeding. I sing
off the cold with American Pop: *come let the rain come down*
                                  let the rain come
                                              come down down

I step over Saturday's youth sprawled drunk on the ground—their
exposed thighs soft moons raising from wet concrete—an eatable
light. I wonder if there is a love beyond consumption. Should have
come   I (sing)   *let the rain*   should have insisted   (sing)
come   on   a condom.

I continue to wonder off years of alone, from church to church
confessing like rain, remembering how your body arched like a
steeple, your voice shucking off cold—in this space, I believed
in more than ten to five, believed in sex as baptism. But now it's, (sing)

come down morning. I'm bleeding, wet, and cold. You're no
walkable distance and I'm out of churches, yet the sleepless
nights keep coming without hope for forgiveness. So I (sing)

never meant sorrow, never meant pain,
let the rain, let the rain, let the rain
                          come down
                                down
                                down.

Notes from Francis D. K. Ching's Architecture Third Edition, Taken from a Mall Food Court

sitting alone—a point has no dimension

           sat in the middle of a mall
           a point is stable and at rest

kitty-   *wheel*
   corner, is a girl in a pin*wheel* hat
         wheel   moved off center, the point becomes more aggressive

                above the girl, in neon, *Hot Dog on a Stick,*
                visual tension is created between the point and its field

a boy leans against her counter—drinks lemonade
two points describe a line that connects—segments of infinity

    his gaze pulled taut against her—an imaginary bird lands on this invisible wire

Vila: Sacrifice

I've given the three fingered G chord
in a golden box— size of my pinkie—
I've given my pinkie—   only to see it
given to another—   art of distancing
affection. I continue to give the wrong
harmonicas to the askew—   in fidelity
of impossibility made possible. I've

done the same to others. Out of our
hands. We are told, it is all out of our
hands.   I rub the center   of my
palm until red wells are dug. Wait for
scabs,   and dig again. Write wants in
red.   Write what we can't   give our-

selves in song; imagine his lips upon
that G
chord—and stains,
size of my hand, rise from this page.

Ravens Fly in Threes

I. To leave the first
love, I had to bury
my younger self—she
didn't go easy. In
my mind, I took her
face with a hatchet—
propped it upright as
a tombstone, continue
to use it as master-
bed's headboard.

II. The second leaving
is a knife that cost me
my entire family. With
kin wedged between
my ribs, the wound
never stops bleeding.

III. For the final love, I
swim out to an imagined
island—watch flies enter
his mouth to eat out
his innards. His caress
turned to a glove, some
days I try to put him on.
I get half dressed in this
skin, before throwing
emptiness to the ground.
I tell my-selves *it's time
to go*; I tell these selves
to *not come back*. I gather

most of me, but some
part always slips back.
He's not coming, I tell
her. *He was never here,*
I tell myself. We were
never a person—just a
place to put himself—
a hole in time: *Let go.*

FROM THE GROUND

I spit three times in
the same spot to
remember seeping.

Red ants gather at
this wet. Their little
arms collect moisture.

Had I touched a lover
with the abandonment
of their drinking, I might

know emptiness. I spit.
Again. I spit and spit,
only to find more spittle.

What I wanted were parameters
     and
an unbinding from self.

        (*Stop lying*) I want (*desire*)

        a home with one wall always burning open,
        a man who behaves as god,
        a mouth
            to transform my body into message.

        Folk-

    lore: wisdom, (*I've buried myself from the waist down.*)
          tradition, (*I've buried myself face first in the ground*)
            experience. (*Who's holding this shovel?*)

WHEN WALL-UP

A bird will find a sky within.

Wall 3 }

Retelling: A Countdown

Son, burn the house that is your mother—let the
flames drift like feathers—
there are stories in this world, beyond all the stones told.

THIRD HOUR OF BEING BURIED ALIVE, THE WIFE THINKS OF HER LAST DAY IN CHURCH: OR SHARP EDGES HIDDEN IN A SEAMSTRESS DRESS

I've a pair
of scissors linked

to my hip by a gold chain—
kneading its edge from under my

bodice—I'm able to pull sharpness
from my neck. It cuts my side. Animal

tracks appear across the white stretch of
my dress. Fox paws on snow banks. I am

becoming red clay. Guarding the blade with
my skirt, I hold its cutting edge in my hands to

beat at mortar boots with the handle. There
is no breaking. What are my options? Could snap

in half—saw my legs off. Instead. I cut a twelve-inch
lock of hair from my head—tie the strands into knots

large as beads. *No devil will take heaven from me*, I hear my-
self say— with a voice that sounds miles outside my mouth.

Stains listen. I throw the blade from my window— its body
chimes on the floor like bells. *The sermon will begin soon as the fox*

is found and the chickens are safe, you said before my final

day in church. The fox found   and gutted—you gave me the skin.
I sewed beads for eyes. Wives were   jealous of its warmth, of their lost
birds. The sermon was on soul—   a substance dense enough to hold

open

rooms. Pews filled with density.   Open   rooms. And beaded eyes unblinking
at the carved wounds in wooden   hands. I prayed in thanks. I prayed
for the hen   I would cut
and pluck and cook with salt and herbs.

Scissors Fall—The Sound Cuts This World in Two

Ding   *Dong*   *Ding*   *Dong*

12

At the End: Day One

Six hours in

I piss myself.

Eight hours more

I shit myself.

What of this is worth fighting for? I wedge myself against
a wall—my second self—and cry her to sleep.

The People

learn to ignore the wife's screams, same
as they seldom notice a bird's singing.

How Rada Began the Practice of Sleeping in Coffins

We build walls higher in one day than
we've been able in three years. Cannot

imagine leaving—possibility—how like
a child to my constructed womb, the wife.

I recognize little of myself—now—not
builder but conduit. How I want to birth

and wed her as my sacred tie to invention.
Rather than leave, I build myself a box—

sleep in a darkness that leads me into
dreaming that I haven't yet been born.

Lulled by the Lullaby of Asthma

I hear Rada sleeping near me—
the measure of his breath is calming;
a pulse of safety—the presence of
protection. I can sleep with him here—
filled with gratitude for his song,
though it is he who buries me alive.

First Night in the Wall, the Wife Begins to Haunt Herself

It is midnight. Daughter sits at the base of the wall
that is me and   sings. I tell her
she's a fool to   wait. I tell her
                    Go home
Refusing to listen, her voice   fills chambers that
exclude me. Each note begins as a lark and swells
to bark.   I can't breathe—   I gasp
out   *little bitch.*   With
pitch she   infuses the whole   until noise
pushes beyond restrictions.   The structure shifts
as an old woman about to collapse—if she folds I
will never see my son again.   I claw at the bricks—
can hardly keep a fainting swell from drowning me.
Mama, she says, *mama.* And song stops with *mama.*
Now that she isn't swallowing all air—I scream,
        the church is falling, and
her feet echo like a mischief of rats from my cellar.

We Would Have Lost the Church

had the wife not yelled out.
At first the voice was not human; I
thought it a demon or it sounded
like many in one—as though she

were all the walls in conversation. It took all my courage to come out of my box, but I did just in time to wedge a loose beam into place—to save the space we'd worked so hard to become.

9

RADA HEARS THE WIFE CRYING

Are you alright?

       (silence)

are you . . .

       I'm fine.

You saved her.

       Who?

The church.

       (silence)

Thank you.

       (silence)

I said . . .

       You're welcome.

THE ONLY OTHER TIME THE WIFE REMEMBERS BEING THANKED

I helped a boy retrieve his kite. Father had taught
me to climb trees; said it might save me from bears.

But there are no bears here, Father, and nothing like
a tree to save me.

I loved to live in upper branches, neither above nor
below, but between worlds. I was thirteen. The kite

was yellow as a meadowlark. When I handed it to
the boy, our fingers touched—blood boiled until

my entire body swelled red as cooked flesh. He
looked at me and said, *Thank you*, then flew away

forever. You are a good man to teach me to climb;
he was a good boy for thanking me. This might be

the extent of all the goodness I will ever full know.

The Morning after for Rada

I. Objective Reality

All seems fine—as all seems to be
fulfilled. But what is that sense of
earth arching its back like a cat in
                defense?

II. Subjective Reality

I've brought you water. I've brought you bread.
What needs healing? What in you hurts? Let me
                mend you.

The Morning after for the Wife

I. Objective Reality

From my window I see the women talking—can see them position
for Rada's attention. Hear them compliment his work, as though I
am not this church. They do not see me as a window—but I am
becoming their only way in or out of these walls.

II. Subjective Reality

Everything hurts, nothing can be fixed. I can
no longer hear my own voice. All echoes of
other women talking about the church I am
becoming. This wall could be any of them,
but I'm the church. I listen to you fuck them
in turns. The ache of what I considered sin,
now sings with life. I fucking hate you more
with each woman who loves the church. I can
hear how they look at you, how each cloaks
you in light—your worth stacking with these
intangible acts of giving. I will never get to
look at you. You will never see me. If I was
ever something more than a wall to anyone,
      I will never know it.

Rada Rada: Rada Is Too Busy to Hear the Wife Call Out the Second Night of Being Buried Alive

The church begins to crack—the sound of glaze burning to glass. This is it then; the concrete solidifies. There will be no getting out after this closure forms. The wife calls out, *Rada, Rada, Rada*

Where are you
when I am becoming?

[silence]

[Realization]

[Say it:]

[Say it you stupid fox:]

He's not coming.

Second Night in the Wall, the Wife Stops Praying and Starts Talking to God

I would deny you, if not for my son's face—
how on my third night as mother, I watched
his features turn to flight—a thousand wings,
motioning a love greater than my body could
contain. Then, and only then, did I believe—
there is a land that extends beyond what can
be expressed—a place surpassing definition,

a home that stands, regardless of how much
weight is stacked upon it. I feel birds stream
from me, gathering, not messages,
but the feelings they contain.

If I could take a pocket of this world with me, it would contain a handful of dirt.

SECOND NIGHT IN THE WALL THE WIFE IS HAUNTED BY THE GHOST SHE IS BECOMING

Again. Midnight. And my daughter's song
is upon me. I watch from my window her
eyes galloping the   distance between us—
a happy skip—   her world rising
and falling with   her every   step.
How can she be   happy? *Wicked
bitch.* Dancing on her mother's last breaths.
                    What do you want?
Mother I have brought you a gift. Mother quick—
catch—   a letter
drops   through
the door at my breast — turns to a dove—
flies about my head.   I catch it   and tear it
with my teeth. Wet salt down my chin. It is
no longer a bird but an envelope.   It is not
flesh but a mouth full of dirt. *For your pocket,*
                    she says.

THE WIFE EATS HER LAST MEAL

In my once empty hand, I find a fist full of earth. I lift it to my face,
smell rain. I fall as a storm. I'm so empty; I eat this dirt and dream
I'm a field of hollyhocks full of *skinwings*, common name, *earwigs.*
They eat me alive, but they are willing to listen to their consumed.

I ask them: If he knew how much this hurts, would he continue to
bury? Insects listen too well; there are no answers. I would ask him
directly, but the idea of *yes*, is far worse than having *no* to cling to. *No.*
He wouldn't continue, if he knew my skin is frail as insect wings.

If he knew, I am; if he knew, I do; he'd know the child-self in me—he
would know that she loves him beyond logic. It's her fault I'm in this
wall; I taught her within, I taught her silence. I didn't want her to hurt,
not like I do, not like I am. If he knew . . . what if he knew? I'm a person.

Would anything change?

Why Husbands Make Terrible Lovers,
Lovers Make Terrible Husbands

She Tells Her Husband,

> I am cold. Rats lick where my fingers bleed. Please.
> Please. A little warmth. A small light. Let me
> see our son, let me feel his breath—that
> wordless language of God—
> against me. Please. Be
> good to me, so I
> can believe in
> goodness
> again.

She Tells Rada the Builder,   At Night

> I can
> hear the
> church grow—
> like blood in my ears
> when my son was in me—
> beat of pulse. I know what is
> needed—what could bring walls
> to the ground. With my little finger, I
> could bury all, but it'd mean killing my son.

Her First as a Wall, the Husband Visits

I brought you our son.

> Show me my son.

He is healthy.

> Not by my breast.

No, your sisters'.

> What sisters?

Please, pity.

> Mercy is not mine.

Please, please, please.

> Unbury me.

> Where is my mother? She will bring a slave for exchange.

Your mother is dead. I cannot bring her to you. May she find you and bring you
peace. Please, make a request I can fulfill. Let me bring you comforts. Let me . . .

> Stop my wretched daughter from ever coming here again.

Please, stop torturing me—we haven't a daughter.

> Don't come here again.

You've gone mad.

> YOU, husband. Useless other, tell Rada the builder,
> this place is built on illusions. He must sever the head
> if the body is to stand. Rada will understand what you
> cannot. Now, leave and don't come back.

The Wife Advises Rada the Builder: We Are Desperate for Answers

We assert
that nature is/
was mathematically
designed—inventing a
key and calling it a door.
Let go of a concrete
foundation—allow
the structure
to open and
shut; as simulacra.
Abstraction   allows
for alternative reality,
that may   (or not) be
of the   real world. I am
becoming   a wall   made
of wings—soon parameters
will morph to pure motion.

Week Two of Construction, Something in Rada Softens

If I were to touch her—
reach into that small door at
her breast and feel her—this
entire   story   would
crumble—what   now   is
stone, would begin to grow
as soft green moss. But how
would I even begin to ask
for permission—to enter?

Under Pressure, Rada Begins to Break

The kings are angry from lack of progress. I could care less for their ideas
of movement.
The youngest king is sent to fetch me.

We look at each other
like foxes over a headless chicken. She, like fault, is ours.
We'd kill each other for the responsibility of feeling—to care and have that care
lead to causation—to be reason contained—with her head in my mouth,
she is more mine than his—I like that he smells this on my breath
as we talk about the church's progress.

The men complain of the cold. Their wives bring them coats and gloves—give them soup and tea. Construction moves slowly—as wives stay—they talk about incontinences; babies who won't sleep, stubborn stains in bedding, a need to patch holes in a wall.

What I hear is:

Children grow by witness, women wash lovemaking to make room for more, homes are cold from neglect; time does not return but overlaps. Making is a taking beyond our control; none of us know the extent of our own losses. I tell the men

go home,

but they stay. I spend the day collecting a bouquet of fallen leaves for the wife in the wall.

THE FIRST PRAYER PRAYED / ANSWERED IN "THE WALLED-UP WIFE"

Stars twist their bodies round. My structure pulses
with light. Down to foundation,   I follow sobbing
as though led by ghosts.   I step softly. Nearly to
her, I see the youngest king at the wall, weeping
forgive me.
His sincerity deserving of any man's pity—he cries
as the fatally injured will bleed.   He cries.
Forgive me,
Lord. How quickly pity turns to disgust. I wonder.
How long have you wished for silence? *Pray God*
never let me be pitied.   When you are tired by
the sound of me,   *God,*   make me silent.

AFTER THE HUSBAND LEAVES, THE WIFE AND BUILDER LEAN AGAINST THEIR SIDE OF THE WALL AND IN SILENCE WONDER IF . . .

. . . she'll ask me to break this wall.

. . . he'll ever know my name.

LAST NIGHT IN THE HOLE:
BECOMING WHOLE

My daughter comes but says nothing.

You aren't real, I say. *But, I know you as*
my daughter. A light flickers. *I would have*
loved you,   light flicker.
Her eyes, blink. *I still love,* I revise.
Unblinking. *You are me,* conclusion. She
slips her   child hand
into the slot of my door—   she enters my
mouth. She   becomes   fine   smoke,
          holding me like sunlight as
                    I let go.

TOO LATE, RADA BREAKS

I wake to a vacancy—silence. The church has stopped its song—
the bones and joints   ossified.
I kick down and out of my sleeping box. I run to the wall, yelling.
No, no, don't go. No.   I take
a hammer to the bricks—they crumble like teeth. Over the heap
of rubble, I see her.   Limp.
Eyes open. She is only a child. I hold her. A child. I choke up my
voice and place it   in her
palm.   Everything for nothing—I know the secrets of the dead.
The living pray the wrong   prayers.

o

Rada Goes to the First Day of Congregation

My breath irregular, I'm worn to the last of a wick,
I hear none

of what is said by the priest. I watch her boy with
those unblinking

eyes, watch light as it sparks on drifts of dirt in air—
shafts like arms

reach into the chapel, stroke his hair—she is here—
she would not

leave without her son, I knew this would be so.
He reaches for

these particles of shine. His father doesn't stop him;
the boy catches

a secondary world—an abstract home that surrounds
and releases him—simultaneously.

This is a home for a love greater than our individual
bodies can hold.

Wall 4

Marginalia

The Only Words Worth Reading Are Written in the Margins

There are nights
when the builder

puts his hand
to the wall

—same night—

the wife puts her
hand to the wall.
They are, one
side reaching for

the other.

Biographical Note

Nicelle Davis is a California poet, collaborator, and performance artist who walks the desert with her son J.J. in search of owl pellets and rattlesnake skins. Her previous collections include *In the Circus of You* (Rose Metal Press, 2015), *Becoming Judas* (Red Hen Press, 2013), and *Circe* (Lowbrow Press, 2011). Her poetry film collaborations with Cheryl Gross have been shown across the world. She has taught poetry at Youth for Positive Change, an organization that promotes success for youth in secondary schools, MHA, Volunteers of America in their Homeless Youth Center, and with Red Hen's WITS program. She runs The Poetry Circus in Los Angeles and The Living Poetry Project. She currently teaches at Paraclete High School. For more about her please visit nicelledavis.net.

Printed in the USA
CPSIA information can be obtained
at www.ICGtesting.com
JSHW060042150824
68134JS00028B/2607